# So, You're Thinking About Becoming a Self-Published Author?

## *A Step-by-Step Guide*

### By Char Vernon

*10-Time Published Author | Speaker | Creative Entrepreneur*

# Dedication

*This book is dedicated to everyone who has a story to tell, a message to share, or knowledge worth putting on paper, but did not know where or how to begin.*

**This is your starting point.**

# Preface

This book was born out of real conversations with real people.

Over the years, as I published one book and then another and then several more, the questions started coming. People who knew me personally, friends, colleagues, and members of my community, would pull me aside and ask: How did you do it? Where do you publish? How did you learn the formatting? How do you design your cover? They were not asking a stranger on the internet. They were asking someone they actually knew, someone they could look in the eye and trust, someone who had done it not once but multiple times.

One conversation in particular stayed with me. A friend came to me and said that he thought I should write a book about how to write a book, and teach classes around it. He said she would be the first to sign up and the first to buy the book. He told me there was nothing out there quite like what I could offer, because most publishing guides are written by people you have never met. This one is written by someone who might be in your circle, your neighborhood, your network. Someone accessible. Someone real.

I had already been thinking about it. I had already been asking people quietly: if I put together a guide on how to self-publish, would you buy it? The answer was always the same. Yes. Every single time.

So I wrote it.

This is not a book full of theory. Everything in these pages comes from my direct personal experience across ten published books, including the mistakes I made, the money I spent fixing those mistakes, and the process I eventually built that works. I am giving you all of it because I do not want you to spend years figuring out what I figured out the hard way.

**You asked. Here is your answer.**

# Acknowledgments

First, I want to thank my creator for the gift of creativity, the discipline to develop it, and the courage to share it with the world.

To every person who has purchased one of my books, left a review, shared kind words, or pulled me aside to tell me how my work impacted them, thank you. You are the reason I keep going. Those conversations, the ones in passing, the messages, the quiet moments where someone said your book helped me, those are what push me forward when the work gets hard. You kept asking questions and your questions became this book.

To my friend Ivan Bethea, thank you for lighting the fire. You have always been to me what I try to be to others, a straight talker, a sound advisor, and someone who believes in the vision before it is fully formed. This book exists in part because of the conversations we have had and the push you gave me to stop thinking about it and start doing it.

And finally, to myself. I want to acknowledge the woman who believed she could do this, who kept going through the learning curves and the mistakes and the moments of doubt, and who showed up anyway. Ten books and counting. This one makes eleven. I am proud of the work and I am proud of the commitment it took to see it through.

**To everyone reading this, your acknowledgment is coming. Write your book.**

# Table of Contents

# Introduction

People ask me all the time how I became a published author. Not just once, but ten times over. They want to know the steps. They want to know what tools I used, how I designed my covers, where I published, and how I made sure my books ended up in places beyond just Amazon. They want the real answer, not the glossed-over version.

This book is that answer. It is the guide I built one hard lesson at a time, and I am giving it to you so you can get it right from the start. Everything in here is based on my direct personal experience. I am only going to tell you what I know, what I have done, and what has worked. Nothing theoretical. Nothing recycled from someone else's process. Just the real steps, in the right order, from someone who has been through it.

Read this book from beginning to end before you start. Then go back and use each chapter as a reference guide as you work through your own publishing journey. The information here is sequential. The decisions you make in Chapter Two affect what happens in Chapter Six. Follow the steps in order and you will save yourself the time, money, and frustration that comes from figuring it out backwards.

Your book is waiting. Let's get it published correctly.

# CHAPTER ONE

# Your Story Starts Here

*How a creative kid with a big imagination became a 10-time published author, and why you are next.*

**Let me be honest with you from the very first page.**

I am not a person who stumbled into publishing by accident. Creativity has been a part of me since I was a child. Writing stories, dreaming up characters, playing with words, and imagining worlds that did not exist yet was just who I was. I had a big imagination and I never let it go. What I did not have, for a long time, was a clear path to turn all of that creativity into something people could hold in their hands. That changed when I published my first book. Then my second. Then my third. Today, as I sit down to write this guide, I am a 10-time published author, and the book you are reading right now will be my eleventh.

I wrote this guide because people ask me all the time: How did you do it? What steps did you follow? Where do you even start? When I started out, there was no one laying it all out for me in plain language. I had to figure it out through trial and error, through mistakes that cost me time and money, and through eventually finding a process that works. This book is everything I wish someone had handed me before I published that first book. Consider it your roadmap.

## It Started With a Child Who Needed More

My journey into publishing did not start with a grand vision or a business plan. It started with my godson and a homework assignment.

I was going over his schoolwork with him one evening and I noticed a gap. There was a deficit between what he was being taught and what I felt a child his age should already know. The basics were there, but the depth was missing. The vocabulary was limited. The words being used to teach the alphabet were the same words that had been used for generations: A for Apple, B for Ball, C for Cat. Simple words. Safe words. But not words that stretched a young mind or built a bigger foundation.

I have always been passionate about the enrichment of children, particularly in urban communities where I have seen firsthand how education can fall short. So instead of just noticing the problem, I decided to do something about it. I created a workbook that challenged children with bigger, more interesting words. Not just A for Apple, but A for Airplane. That workbook became my very first published book: Practice Makes Perfect, Alphabetical Tracing Workbook. It was not perfect. It was my first attempt and I was absolutely dipping my toe in the water. But it was mine, it was real, and it was on the page.

## Creativity Runs in the Family

I will tell you something else that pushed me in this direction. My mother is also an author. She has published children's books of her own. Growing up with a mother who believed that stories matter, that words have power, and that you do not have to wait for someone else to tell your story, that environment shaped how I see the world. I am not one to share personal details publicly, but I will say this: if you have someone in your life who has already done something you want to do, pay attention to them. Let their example be your proof that it is possible.

My mother's example told me it was possible. My godson's homework told me it was necessary. And my own creativity told me it was time.

## From One Book to Ten

After Practice Makes Perfect, I kept going. I asked myself a simple question: what do I know, and who needs to know it? The answer turned out to be a long list.

I know children's stories. I know how to play with words, build characters, and create books that grab the attention of young readers. So I kept writing children's books. Brandon's Brave Biking Bonanza. The Curious Adventures of Kiki in the Kitchen. A to Z: A Day at the Park with Friends. Ava's Amazing Alphabet Adventure. Each one was an exercise in wordplay and imagination. My long-term goal is to become what I call the urban Dr. Seuss, an author who plays with language, gets creative with words, and writes stories that reflect the world urban children actually live in. That vision keeps growing with every book.

But I did not stop at children's books. I have 25 years of professional experience in human resources. People come to me constantly for career advice, workplace guidance, and professional development. So I wrote about that too. Navigating the Workforce While Black in America speaks directly to the challenges that so many professionals face but rarely see addressed in print. The Struggles in Today's Job Market tackles what workers are up against right now in a shifting economy. Launch and Thrive: Step by Step Side Hustle Guide is for the person who has a vision for something bigger and needs a clear starting point.

And then there is the personal development side of who I am. I am a firm believer in manifestation, in the power of habits, and in the idea that your mindset shapes your reality. Make That Sh*t Happen: 30 Day Good Habits Journal and Manifest Like a Misfit: A 30-Day Manifestation

Journal both came from that place. They are the books I wrote for the person who is ready to stop waiting and start doing.

Ten books. Five children's titles. Five adult titles covering careers, self-help, and personal development. All written from lived experience. All self-published. All mine.

## Why I Wrote This Guide

Here is the thing about self-publishing that nobody tells you up front: the writing is the easy part. Once the words are on the page, you still have to figure out how to turn those words into a real book. You have to understand cover design, interior formatting, ISBNs, publishing platforms, pricing, and distribution. You have to make decisions that will either give you full control over your work or quietly hand that control over to someone else.

I made mistakes along the way. Some of those mistakes cost me real time and real money to fix. I published books on the wrong platform, used the wrong ISBN, and had to go back and redo things that I could have done correctly from the start if I had simply known better. I am sharing all of that in this guide, including what I did wrong and exactly how to avoid making the same mistakes.

This guide is for the person who has a story to tell and does not know where to start. It is for the professional who wants to package their expertise into a book. It is for the parent or teacher who sees a gap in the resources available to children and wants to fill it. It is for the creative person who has been sitting on an idea for years, waiting for the right moment or the right permission. Consider this your permission.

## How to Use This Book

Each chapter of this guide covers one specific part of the self-publishing process, in the order you will actually need it. Start at the beginning and work your way through. If you are enrolled in the companion course, each chapter maps directly to a lesson. Use this as your reference guide before, during, and long after the course ends.

I have published ten books and I am still learning. But I can tell you this with complete confidence: once you publish your first book, everything changes. You stop being a person who wants to write a book and you become an author. That shift is real, it is powerful, and it is waiting for you on the other side of the work.

### *Let's get started.*

### Chapter Reflection: Know Your Why

Before you move on to Chapter Two, take a few minutes to answer these questions.

**1. Why do you want to publish a book?**

______________________________________________________

______________________________________________________

**2. Who is your book for?**

______________________________________________________

______________________________________________________

**3. What has stopped you from moving forward until now?**

______________________________________________________

______________________________________________________

**4. What would it mean to you to hold your published book in your hands?**

# CHAPTER TWO

# Before You Write a Word, Know Your Book

*The decisions you make before you start writing will determine everything that comes after.*

**Most people think the hardest part of writing a book is the writing. It is not.**

The hardest part is knowing what you are writing before you start. Before you open Canva, before you think about your cover, before you look up a single thing about ISBNs or publishing platforms, you need to answer one fundamental question: what is this book, and who is it for?

## Start With the Topic, Not the Title

One of the first things I do when I am thinking about a new book is identify the topic and ask myself why it matters right now. Not why it matters to me personally, but why it matters to the person who is going to pick it up and read it.

For my children's books, the topic almost always comes from something I observe. For my adult books, the topic usually comes from conversations. Real ones. I have 25 years of experience in human resources and people ask me questions constantly. For my journals and manifestation books, the topic comes from self-reflection. I look at what I am personally working on and what tools have actually helped me grow.

> *Every book starts with a clear topic, a reason it needs to exist, and an honest answer to the question of who it is written for. Get that right first and the rest becomes much easier.*

## The Most Common Mistake First-Time Authors Make

The most common mistake I see before people even put a single word on the page is this: they want to write a book about themselves.

There is a difference between writing from your experience and writing about yourself. One serves the reader. The other serves the author. A person who does not know you is not going to buy your book because of what happened to you. They are going to buy it because of what it is going to do for them.

The books I have written that connect most with readers are the ones that are technically about my experience but are actually written for someone else's situation. Write from your experience. But write for your reader.

> *Write from your experience. But write for your reader. That is the line between a book that sits in a drawer and a book that actually sells.*

## Know What You Want Your Reader to Walk Away With

Every book I have published has a lesson in it. Before you write your book, I want you to be able to finish this sentence clearly: When someone finishes reading this book, they will know how to _______________, or they will feel _______________, or they will be able to _______________.

If you cannot finish that sentence, you are not ready to start writing yet. Sit with it. Because once you have that answer, your entire book has a north star to navigate by.

## Choose Your Genre and Know What It Requires

Children's books are shorter, heavily visual, and usually built around a single concept or story arc. I focus primarily on children between the ages of 6 and 12 because that is the window where core reading and vocabulary skills are being built.

Nonfiction books are organized around information. They have chapters, sections, and a logical flow that takes the reader from where they are to where they want to be. Journals and workbooks are a hybrid. They combine instructional content with space for the reader to respond, reflect, and take action.

## How to Build Your Outline

For nonfiction, I start by writing down every question I think my reader might have about the topic. Then I group those questions into themes. Each theme becomes a chapter. Within each chapter, I map out the key points I need to cover to fully answer those questions. That structure becomes my outline, and my outline becomes my book.

> *Your outline does not have to be perfect. It just has to give you a direction. Starting without one is one of the fastest ways to get lost.*

## Set a Realistic Goal for Length

Your book needs to be as long as it takes to fully deliver on the promise you made to your reader, and not one page longer. Do not pad your book to make it feel more substantial. Readers can tell. And do not cut it short because you ran out of energy. If you made a promise on the cover, fulfill it on every page.

*Know your topic. Know your reader. Know your takeaway. Everything else is details.*

## Chapter Reflection: Map Your Book

**1. What is your book about? Write your topic in one clear sentence.**

_______________________________________________

_______________________________________________

**2. Who is your reader? Be specific about age, situation, or background.**

_______________________________________________

_______________________________________________

**3. Complete this sentence: When someone finishes reading my book, they will _____________________.**

_______________________________________________

_______________________________________________

**4. What genre is your book?**

_______________________________________________

_______________________________________________

**5. List your chapter topics or main sections below. Aim for at least five.**

_______________________________________________

_______________________________________________

_______________________________________________

_______________________________________________

_______________________________________________

_______________________________________________

# CHAPTER THREE

# Designing Your Book Cover

*Your cover is not decoration. It is your first and most powerful marketing tool.*

**Your cover has one job: make a stranger stop and pick up your book.**

It does not matter how good the writing is inside if the cover does not do that job first. I design all of my covers myself using Canva Pro, and over the course of ten books I have developed a process that works. This chapter will walk you through that process step by step.

## The Most Important Thing Nobody Tells You First

Before you design a single element of your cover, you need to finish your manuscript. Your cover dimensions are determined by two things: the size of your book and the number of pages in your manuscript. The number of pages determines the thickness of your spine. If you design your cover before your manuscript is complete, your cover template will be wrong and you will have to redo it. Finish the manuscript first. Then generate your cover template. Then design your cover.

> *Finish your manuscript first. Generate your cover template second. Design your cover third. Do not skip steps.*

## A Time-Saving Tip: Set Your Word Document to Book Size First

Set your Word document to your book dimensions before you start formatting your manuscript. In Microsoft Word, go to Layout, then Size, then More Paper Sizes. In the width field type 6.69 and in the height field type 9.61. Click OK. Your document is now the exact size of your finished book. When you bring that content into Canva Pro at those same dimensions, the text will flow much more predictably and require far less reformatting.

There is also another option: once your Word document is formatted at the correct book dimensions, you can export it directly from Word as a PDF and upload that PDF straight to IngramSpark as your interior file, skipping Canva for the interior entirely. Canva would then only be used for the cover.

> *Set your Word document to 6.69 x 9.61 inches before you start formatting. It will save you hours of reformatting time.*

## Choosing Your Book Dimensions

My standard size for books and journals is 6.69 x 9.61 inches. This is what I use in Canva Pro for all of my adult titles and journals. For workbooks, I use 8.5 x 11 inches because the larger page gives the reader more room to write and interact with the content. These are two distinct formats for two distinct products.

## Understanding Your Cover: Front, Back, and Spine

Your cover is one continuous piece that wraps around the entire book. It has three parts: the front cover, the spine, and the back cover. All three are designed together as a single file. The spine width is determined by your page count. A book with 100 pages has a very thin spine. This is exactly why your manuscript must be finished before you generate your cover template.

The back cover is where you put your book description. It may also include a short author bio, any endorsements, and the barcode area for your ISBN. The barcode placement has a designated area on the back cover and needs to be left clear in your design.

## How to Generate Your Cover Template From IngramSpark

### Step 1: Go to IngramSpark's cover template generator.

IngramSpark has a free tool on their website for generating book cover templates. You do not need an account to use it.

### Step 2: Enter your book details.

The generator will ask for your trim size, interior paper color, and page count. Enter the exact information from your finished manuscript.

### Step 3: Enter your ISBN.

Enter the Bowker ISBN assigned to this book. Do not use a placeholder.

### Step 4: Download your template.

IngramSpark will generate a PDF template showing the exact dimensions of your full cover including the safe zones and barcode area.

### Step 5: Take the dimensions into Canva Pro.

Open Canva Pro and create a new custom-size design using the exact dimensions from your template.

## Designing Your Cover in Canva Pro

I start with a concept. What do I want this cover to communicate? Then I may look at templates in Canva Pro for inspiration, but I never use a template as-is. I always change it. The template is just a starting point. The final design is always something different from what I started with.

Canva Pro gives you access to a large library of royalty-free images and illustrations included with your subscription. With Canva Pro's built-in AI image generation, you can take an existing character or image and generate variations of it. That capability has changed the game significantly for independent authors who cannot afford a professional illustrator.

> *If you are going to use Canva to design your books professionally, invest in Canva Pro. The free version will limit you in ways that will show up in your final product.*

## Use YouTube as Your Best Resource

Even after designing ten book covers, I still go to YouTube when I run into something I cannot figure out in Canva. These platforms update constantly. YouTube is always current. If you have never used Canva before, go to YouTube first and search for how to design a book cover in Canva Pro. Watch a few videos before you start.

> *YouTube is free, it is current, and it has tutorials for nearly every specific task you will ever need to do in Canva. Use it without shame.*

## Exporting Your Cover Correctly

When your cover is complete, click Download and select PDF Print. Always check the box for crop marks and bleed. For color profile, CMYK is the standard for professional printing. RGB is the default and works fine in most cases. Either way, always select crop marks and bleed before you hit download.

You will have two separate files to upload to IngramSpark: one for your cover and one for your manuscript interior. You do not need to manually add a barcode to your design. If you have purchased your own ISBN and entered it during the IngramSpark setup, IngramSpark will automatically place the barcode on your back cover. Simply leave that area clean.

*Your cover is the first conversation your book has with a reader. Make it count.*

## Chapter Reflection: Plan Your Cover

1. What trim size have you chosen for your book and why?

\
\

2. What feeling or mood do you want your cover to communicate?

\
\

3. What colors, images, or design elements are you thinking about?

\
\

4. Write a first draft of your back cover blurb below.

\
\
\
\

# CHAPTER FOUR

# Building the Inside of Your Book

*Every page inside your book has a purpose. This chapter tells you what goes where and why.*

**A professional book is not just well written. It is well organized.**

When a reader opens your book, before they read a single word of your actual content, they are already forming an impression based on how your interior is put together. This chapter walks you through the interior of a professionally formatted book, page by page, in the exact order they should appear.

## The Page-by-Page Interior Structure

### Page 1: Title Page

Your full book title, subtitle if you have one, and your name as the author. Keep it clean and simple.

### Page 2: Blank Page

A single blank page follows the title page. This is standard in professional book formatting.

### Page 3: Copyright Page

Your copyright notice with year and name, all rights reserved statement, your ISBN, edition number, and country of printing.

### Page 4: Dedication Page

A brief, heartfelt acknowledgment. One to three sentences is standard.

### Page 5: Preface

Written in your voice. Tells the reader why you wrote this book. This is where your credibility lives.

### Page 6: Acknowledgments Page

Thank the people who helped make the book possible.

### Page 7: Table of Contents

Lists every chapter and major section with corresponding page numbers.

### Page 8: Introduction

Sets up the content, tells the reader what they will learn, and prepares them for the chapters ahead.

### Page 9: Blank Page

Insert one blank page before Chapter One begins.

### Page 10+: Chapter One and Beyond

This is where your page numbering begins. Page one is the first page of Chapter One. Every page from this point forward carries a page number.

### After final chapter: Blank Page

Insert one blank page after your final numbered content page.

### Final pages: About the Author

Your author bio page with a professional photo and a paragraph about your background and credentials.

### Closing: Blank Page or Pages as Needed

Add blank pages as needed to bring your total page count to an even number. IngramSpark requires an even page count.

> *Do not skip the front matter pages because they seem optional. They are what separate a professional publication from a document someone printed at home.*

## The Copyright Page: What to Include

- Copyright symbol, year, and your full legal name. Example: Copyright 2025 Char Vernon

- All rights reserved statement.

- Your ISBN from Bowker assigned to this specific book and format.
- Edition information. Example: First Edition, 2025.
- Country of printing. Example: Printed in the United States of America.

Important: The ISBN on your copyright page and the ISBN you enter into IngramSpark must match exactly. Confirm this before you submit.

## Page Numbers: Where They Start

Page numbers start on page one of Chapter One. The front matter pages do not carry page numbers in the standard numbering sequence. Your table of contents should be one of the last things you finalize, after all chapters are written and page numbers are set.

> *Page numbers start at Chapter One. Front matter is not numbered. Finalize your table of contents last.*

## Fonts, Font Sizes, and Formatting Standards

For my book interiors, I use Calibri as my standard body font. It is clean, professional, and easy to read on a printed page. For font size, I stay between 11 and 12 point for body text. A font size below 10 point is too small for comfortable reading. Maintain consistent spacing throughout your document.

> *Readable is the goal. Use a clean font, a comfortable size, and consistent spacing throughout.*

## Writing Your Author Bio Page

Your bio page should include a professional photo, a paragraph about your background and credentials, a mention of your other published works, and any professional experience relevant to the book. How personal you get is entirely your choice. My preference is to share what is relevant without revealing details I consider private. There are no strict rules about what you must include. The only rule is that whatever you include should be true and should serve the reader's understanding of why you are qualified to have written this book.

## The Even Page Count Rule

Before you submit your interior file to IngramSpark, confirm that your total page count is an even number. If the number is odd, add one blank page at the very end. This is also why you should do a final page count before you generate your cover template, since your spine width is calculated based on your page count.

> *Always confirm an even page count before submitting to IngramSpark. Then confirm your cover template still matches your updated page count.*

*A well-built interior is invisible to the reader. They should never notice the formatting. They should only notice the content.*

## Chapter Reflection: Interior Checklist

- Title page is complete.
- Blank page follows the title page.
- Copyright page includes all required information including your ISBN.
- Dedication page is written.
- Preface is written in your voice.
- Acknowledgments page is complete.
- Table of contents lists all chapters with accurate page numbers.

- Introduction is written.

- Blank page is inserted before Chapter One.

- Page numbers begin at Chapter One.

- Blank page is inserted after the final numbered page.

- Author bio page with photo is complete.

- Total page count is an even number.

- Interior has been exported as a PDF Print file and reviewed in full.

# CHAPTER FIVE

# Your ISBN: Own It, Do Not Borrow It

*One number changes everything about where your book can go and who controls it.*

**I am going to give you the game right here, because this is the chapter I wish had existed before I published my first book.**

An ISBN is a 13-digit number that identifies your book. It is what makes your book findable in databases, bookstores, libraries, school systems, and distribution networks worldwide. What most first-time self-published authors do not know is that where you get your ISBN from determines almost everything about what you can do with your book after it is published.

## How I Found Out I Was Doing It Wrong

My turning point came when I started looking into how to get my books into bookstores. I had published several books through KDP using their free ISBN. When I researched getting my books into physical stores and school systems, I kept hitting a wall. The answer kept coming back to the same thing: I needed my own ISBN. Not a borrowed one. Not a free one assigned by a platform. My own.

I am big on education and I want my books, particularly my children's titles and the curriculums I am developing, to be available in schools. For that to happen, I needed to be recognized as a legitimate independent publisher. Once I understood what was at stake, the decision was simple.

## The Difference Between a Free KDP ISBN and Your Own Bowker ISBN

When you publish through KDP and use their free ISBN, Amazon is listed as the publisher of record for your book. Your book is tied to their platform. You cannot take that book with its KDP ISBN and distribute it through IngramSpark, place it in bookstores, or submit it to school systems and libraries through proper distribution channels.

There is also another layer most people do not know. When you publish through KDP using their ISBN and their platform terms, you are giving Amazon significant rights over your book. Many authors do not fully realize this until they try to do something with their book outside of Amazon and discover they cannot.

When you purchase your own ISBN through Bowker, you are the publisher of record. You own the book entirely. You can publish it on IngramSpark, distribute it through multiple channels, and submit it to schools, libraries, and bookstores.

> *A free ISBN from KDP makes Amazon your publisher. Your own ISBN from Bowker makes you your own publisher. The difference is everything.*

## How to Purchase Your ISBN Through Bowker

Bowker is the official ISBN agency for the United States. Their website is myidentifiers.com. You will see different bundle options. If you have any intention of writing more than one book, buy in bulk. I purchased a bundle of 10 ISBNs and it was significantly more cost-effective per ISBN than buying them one at a time. Visit the site to see current pricing before you purchase.

## What Bowker Will Ask You When You Assign Your ISBN

When you go into Bowker to assign your ISBN to your book title, they will ask you to fill in some basic information about your book. Have the following ready before you start: your full book title and subtitle, your name as the author, your publication date, a book description of up to 350 words, your genre and subject category, your target audience, and your retail price. This is the same information you will enter in IngramSpark, so if you have it prepared in advance the process on both platforms will go much faster. None of these fields are complicated but having your answers ready before you sit down will save you time and keep you from getting stuck in the middle of the process.

## How to Use Your ISBNs

When you purchase a bundle of ISBNs from Bowker, you do not have to assign them to a book immediately. You can hold onto them until you are ready to use them. Each book title gets its own ISBN. If you write ten books, you need ten ISBNs, one for each title. It is one ISBN per book, not one per format. If you publish the same book as both a print copy and a digital version, that is still one book and one ISBN covers it.

I personally publish print copies of my books. I have not gone through the process of publishing eBooks, so I am not going to walk you through something I have not done myself. Everything I am teaching you in this book is based on my direct personal experience with print publishing.

## What Owning Your ISBN Actually Gets You

When you publish through IngramSpark with your own ISBN, your book enters IngramSpark's global distribution network. It becomes available for bookstores, libraries, schools, and other retailers to order. However, being available through IngramSpark's distribution network does not mean your book will automatically appear on the physical shelves of your local bookstore. Distribution makes your book orderable. Getting it onto a physical shelf is a separate process that involves reaching out to stores directly.

> *Your own ISBN opens the doors. It does not walk you through them automatically. But you cannot get through doors that are locked, and KDP's free ISBN keeps most of them locked.*

## The One Thing I Wish I Had Known First

If I could go back to before I published my very first book and tell myself one thing, it would be this: buy your ISBNs before you do anything else. Because the ISBN is the foundation that everything else is built on. It is what gives you ownership. It is what gives you options. Get your ISBNs first. Own your work from day one.

---

***Own your ISBN. Own your book. Own your future as an author.***

---

## Chapter Reflection: Your ISBN Action Steps

- Go to myidentifiers.com and review the current ISBN bundle options.

- Decide how many ISBNs you need based on how many books you plan to publish.

- Purchase your ISBNs and save them somewhere accessible.

- If you have already published books using a KDP free ISBN, make a list of those titles and plan your republishing strategy.

**How many books do you plan to publish?**

_______________________________________________________

_______________________________________________________


**Which ISBN bundle makes the most sense for your goals?**

_______________________________________________________

_______________________________________________________


**Do you have any books already published under a KDP ISBN that need to be moved?**

_______________________________________________________

_______________________________________________________

# CHAPTER SIX

# Skip KDP. Start With IngramSpark.

*I did it backwards so you do not have to. Here is the right way to publish from day one.*

**Let me tell you what I did wrong so you can do it right.**

When I first started publishing, I went straight to KDP. I published several books there, used their free ISBN, and got my books on Amazon. For a while I thought that was enough. It was not. And fixing what I had done the wrong way cost me time and energy I could have spent building my catalog. The right place to start is IngramSpark. Not KDP.

## Why IngramSpark First, Every Time

When you publish your book on IngramSpark, it automatically becomes available on Amazon. You do not need a KDP account. IngramSpark distributes your book to Amazon as part of its standard distribution network, along with Barnes and Noble online, libraries, schools, and other retail and institutional channels worldwide.

When you start with IngramSpark and your own Bowker ISBN, you get Amazon plus every other door that is open to independently published authors. When you start with KDP and their free ISBN, you get Amazon and essentially nothing else.

*IngramSpark distributes to Amazon automatically. You do not need KDP to be on Amazon. But you do need IngramSpark to be everywhere else.*

## What to Have Ready Before You Start

IngramSpark is not difficult but it is strict. Have everything prepared and correct before you begin.

- Your finished interior manuscript exported as a PDF Print file at your correct book dimensions.

- Your finished cover file exported as a PDF Print file with crop marks and bleed selected.

- Your Bowker ISBN assigned to this specific book title.

- Your book title, subtitle, and author name exactly as they appear on your cover.

- Your book description.

- Your genre and subject categories.

- Your banking and tax information for payment setup.

## The Step-by-Step Book Setup Process

### Step 1: Start a new title.

From your IngramSpark dashboard, select the option to add a new title. Enter your title, subtitle, author name, and ISBN. This is also a good moment to confirm that this same ISBN is printed on the copyright page inside your manuscript. The ISBN on your copyright page and the ISBN you enter into IngramSpark must match exactly.

### Step 2: Enter your book details.

Enter your book description, genre and subject categories, and publication date. Your description is what potential readers and buyers will see in catalog listings. Take your time here.

### Step 3: Select your print specifications.

Enter your trim size, interior paper color, and binding type. Any mismatch between your file specifications and what you enter here will cause errors during review.

### Step 4: Upload your interior file.

Upload your manuscript PDF. IngramSpark will run an automated check. Fix any flagged issues and re-upload before moving forward.

### Step 5: Upload your cover file.

Upload your cover PDF. The most common cover issue is spine dimensions. Always confirm your final page count before generating your cover template.

### Step 6: Set your pricing and distribution.

Set your retail price and wholesale discount. A standard wholesale discount is around 55 percent. Make sure your retail price accounts for production cost, the wholesale discount, and still leaves you a reasonable royalty.

### Step 7: Review and submit.

Do a final review of everything before you submit. Once you submit, IngramSpark will do a full manual review that typically takes a few business days.

> *IngramSpark is strict, not hard. Come in prepared with clean files and accurate information and the process is straightforward.*

## The Spine Issue: What Kept Tripping Me Up

Most of my books are under 150 pages, which means a very thin spine. At a low page count, there may not be enough room to put readable text on the spine. In that case the spine can simply be left blank or filled with a solid color. I kept designing my cover with spine text and then discovering the spine was too narrow to hold it. Generate the IngramSpark template first. Build your cover around those exact dimensions.

> *Generate your IngramSpark cover template first, then design your cover around it. Never design first and hope the template matches.*

## What Happens After You Submit

Once your book passes review, it enters IngramSpark's distribution network. It becomes available for Amazon, Barnes and Noble online, libraries, schools, and other retailers to find and order. Getting physically stocked in a store is a separate process. IngramSpark makes your book available and orderable. Getting it onto a physical shelf is outreach work you do yourself.

## If You Already Published on KDP: How to Fix It

Go into your KDP account and unpublish the book. Purchase your own ISBN from Bowker. Assign that ISBN to the book. Reformat your files if needed. Then publish on IngramSpark with your own ISBN. Once IngramSpark distributes your book it will appear on Amazon through IngramSpark's distribution channel.

*Start with IngramSpark. Own your ISBN. Let the distribution work for you.*

## Chapter Reflection: Your Publishing Checklist

- Manuscript is complete, formatted correctly, and exported as a PDF Print file.
- Total page count is confirmed as an even number.
- IngramSpark cover template has been generated using the final page count.
- Cover is designed in Canva Pro using the IngramSpark template dimensions.
- Cover is exported as a PDF Print file with crop marks and bleed selected.
- Bowker ISBN is purchased and assigned to this book title.
- Book description is written and ready to paste into IngramSpark.
- Banking and tax information is ready for account setup.

- All files and information have been reviewed for accuracy before submission.

# CHAPTER SEVEN

# Pricing, Royalties, and Getting Paid

*Pricing your book is not a guess. It is a business decision based on the market, your costs, and what your reader is willing to pay.*

**You wrote the book. Now let's make sure you actually get paid fairly for it.**

## How to Price Your Book: Start With the Market

The first thing I do when figuring out what to charge for a book is look at what similar books are already selling for. Go to a bookstore. Walk the aisles. Look at books in your genre and your category. Look at the price on the back cover. Then go online and do the same on Amazon and Barnes and Noble.

A children's book typically runs between $7.99 and $14.99 in a bookstore setting. Based on my own experience across both children's books and adult titles, I consider $11.99 to $18.99 to be a safe and reasonable pricing range for most independently published books. Where you land within that range depends on your page count, your genre, your audience, and what comparable titles are selling for.

> *Do not guess at your price. Walk into a bookstore, look at comparable titles, and let the market tell you what readers already expect to pay.*

## Understanding the Royalty Split

When you publish through IngramSpark, the revenue is split between you, IngramSpark, and the retailer or distributor who sells the book. When you set up your book in IngramSpark, the platform will show you a breakdown of how your royalty is calculated based on the retail price you set and the wholesale discount you offer. Read that breakdown carefully before you finalize your price.

As a general reference point, the split is often discussed around a 60-40 range, though the exact amount depends on your retail price, production costs, and wholesale discount setting. IngramSpark is transparent about this during setup and will show you the math before you commit.

> *IngramSpark shows you exactly what you will earn per copy before you finalize your price. Use that tool. Adjust your price until the royalty feels right, then commit.*

## When and How You Get Paid

IngramSpark pays you your royalties on a monthly basis. If you sell one book in April, you will receive the royalty for that one book in your next payment cycle. Your royalties are deposited directly to the bank account you set up during the IngramSpark account creation process. Always check IngramSpark's current payment terms directly on their website to confirm the specifics for your account.

## Selling Your Own Copies Directly: The Higher Margin Strategy

When you sell a book through IngramSpark, a portion goes to the platform and a portion goes to the retailer. But when you order copies at the author or bulk pricing IngramSpark offers and sell those copies yourself at events, speaking engagements, pop-up markets, or through your own website, you keep the full retail price minus only what you paid for the copy. That margin is significantly higher.

Bundling your book with a course or workshop is another powerful strategy. When someone enrolls in your course and receives the book as part of the package, you are not splitting that sale with anyone.

## A Safe Pricing Framework

Children's books: Market range is generally $7.99 to $14.99. Aim for the middle to upper end for a professionally produced independent title.

Adult nonfiction, self-help, and career books: Market range is generally $12.99 to $24.99. For most independently published titles, $14.99 to $18.99 is a comfortable and credible price point.

Journals and workbooks: These can be priced similarly to adult nonfiction or slightly higher if they are substantial in size and content.

*Know the market. Understand the split. Price your work like the professional you are.*

## Chapter Reflection: Set Your Price

**1. What do comparable titles in your category sell for?**

_______________________________________________________

_______________________________________________________

**2. What retail price are you considering and what will your royalty be at that price?**

_______________________________________________________

_______________________________________________________

**3. How many copies could you realistically sell directly at events in your first year?**

_______________________________________________________

_______________________________________________________

# CHAPTER EIGHT

# Marketing Your Book: People Cannot Buy What They Cannot Find

*Publishing your book is the beginning, not the finish line. The real work starts the moment it goes live.*

**Your book is not on sale just because it exists.**

Publishing puts your book in the world. Marketing is what brings the world to your book. If you are not actively telling people about your book, consistently and creatively, it will sit there quietly while you wonder why it is not selling. I am an introvert. My approach to marketing is different from what you will read in most author marketing guides. But I have still found ways to move books, get attention, and build momentum. Give yourself at least six months to a year to properly market one book. That is the reality.

## Start With the People Who Already Know You

The first place I always start is with the people already in my life. A significant number of my early book sales came from people at my job who found out I had published and wanted to support. Do not underestimate how powerful your existing network is.

Post about your book on your personal social media pages. Create short video clips, reels, or snippet videos that show the cover and share what the book is about. Post those on YouTube, share them in Facebook groups, put them on Instagram. Repetition matters in marketing. People need to see something multiple times before they act on it.

## Keep Books on You at All Times

I order author copies of my books at a discounted rate through IngramSpark and I keep them in my car. Always. Everywhere I go is a potential sales opportunity. When you have a physical copy of your book with you, it becomes real to people in a way that a link or a social media post never can. I have given books away and I have sold books out of my trunk. Both are valid strategies.

## Book Signings and Local Business Partnerships

Some of my most effective book signing opportunities came from walking into local coffee shops and tea shops with my books and simply asking if they would be open to hosting an author. Many small businesses are happy to do this because it brings traffic to their location. These informal signings also give you the chance to sell copies directly, which means you keep significantly more of the money than you would from a platform sale.

## Use Your Community Platforms

One platform that worked well for me and that most authors overlook is Nextdoor, the neighborhood-based social network. People on Nextdoor are local, community-minded, and often looking to support people in their area. Facebook groups are another underutilized resource. Find the groups where your target reader already spends time and show up there consistently.

## Get Creative: The Press Kit and the Outreach Letter

I created a press kit, also called a press sell sheet, for my books. A press sell sheet is a one-page professional document that includes your book cover image, a brief description, your author bio, your contact information, and ordering details. You can create one in Canva Pro. I have taken my press kit and a copy of my book directly to bookstores.

Let me be real about what that process looks like. I reached out to a prominent independent bookstore that focuses on Black authors. The waiting list just to get a meeting was eight months. That is not a discouragement. That is a reality check. Getting your book into physical stores takes patience, persistence, and a professional presentation.

Another outreach strategy I used for one of my career books was writing letters directly to congresspeople and public figures whose work was relevant to the subject matter. I sent a physical copy of the book along with a letter and my bio. It was a bold move and it got responses, including one from the president.

> *A press kit makes you look like a professional. A bold outreach letter gets you in rooms you might not otherwise access. Both cost almost nothing and can open significant doors.*

## Turn Your Book Into Content

One of the most creative things I have done to market a book is turn it into a free animated video on YouTube. I used Canva Pro's presentation and video export feature to create an animated version of Brandon's Brave Biking Bonanza and uploaded it to YouTube for free. The video gives people a taste of the book and the purchase link is right there in the description. This strategy works because it meets people where they already are.

## What to Avoid: The Author Groups Trap

There are a lot of author groups on social media where authors promote their books to each other. My honest assessment is that most of them are not effective for driving sales. Everyone in those groups is also an author trying to sell a book. You are not reaching readers. You are reaching other writers who are focused on their own work. Your time is better spent going to the places where your actual reader lives.

> *Market to your reader, not to other authors. Find the communities where your target audience already spends time and show up there consistently.*

## The Long Game: What Marketing Really Looks Like

It is not a launch day spike that sustains itself. It is consistent, ongoing effort over months and years. It is keeping books in your car. It is posting regularly even when engagement feels low. It is following up with that bookstore after six months on the waiting list. Give yourself at least six months to a year to properly market each book. The authors who stay consistent are the ones who build a catalog that keeps selling long after the initial launch energy has faded.

---

***Be your own advocate. Get creative. Stay consistent. The book will not sell itself.***

---

## Chapter Reflection: Your Marketing Plan

**1. Who are the first 10 people in your network you will tell about your book?**

2.  What local businesses or community spaces could you approach about a book signing?

3.  Where does your target reader spend time online?

4.  What creative content could you make around your book?

5.  Who are three public figures or organizations you could send an outreach letter and a copy of your book to?

# CHAPTER NINE

# What Comes After: Building a Body of Work

*One book is a start. A catalog is a legacy. Here is what happens when you keep going.*

**You made it to the last chapter. Now let's talk about what happens next.**

Everything in this book up to this point has been about getting your first book published correctly. But the question I want to answer in this final chapter is what happens after you do all of that. What does it look like when you keep going?

## What Publishing Your First Book Actually Does for You

Anybody can have a resume. Anybody can say they have experience, that they have knowledge, that they are an expert in something. But when you can take everything you know and convey it into something that people can read, study, and learn from, it changes the way the world receives you.

After I published my first book, people began to see my credentials differently. Not because my knowledge had changed, but because I had done something with it that was visible and tangible and lasting. A book builds credibility in a way that a job title or a degree alone cannot. Publishing increased my confidence, my visibility, and the level of respect I receive when I speak about my areas of expertise.

> *Anyone can claim expertise. A published book proves it. It is the most powerful professional credential most people never think to create.*

## What I Know Now That I Did Not Know After Book One

People often ask me if publishing gets easier the more you do it. The honest answer is yes and no. The process becomes more familiar. After seven or eight books I had finally internalized the formatting, the dimensions, the IngramSpark workflow, and all the details that used to slow me down. But something is always changing. Platforms update. Tools evolve. The market shifts. You never fully arrive at a place where you can stop paying attention.

What I really know now is this: the knowledge I had to work seven books to acquire, you now have access to in the first chapter of this guide. That is the whole point.

> *The process gets more familiar with every book. But something is always changing. Stay curious, stay current, and never assume you already know everything.*

## Keep Writing: The Outline Is Your Lifeline

For the person who is sitting on a book idea and has not started yet, or who has started and keeps getting stuck, here is one piece of practical advice that will make the biggest difference: build your outline and give yourself a hard stop.

When you write without a structure, you can write and write and never know when you are done. An outline gives you a destination. It tells you what needs to be covered and in what order, and it tells you when you are finished. When you reach the end of your outline, stop. That is your book. Perfectionism is one of the biggest reasons books never get finished. At some point you have to decide the book is complete and move it forward.

## Where Publishing Has Taken Me: Curriculums and the Next Chapter

As I write this, I am in the process of developing educational curriculums. This is the next evolution of everything I have been building as an author and it is rooted in the same passion that drove me to write my first book: the enrichment of young people and the belief that education done well can change the trajectory of a life.

Developing a curriculum is a completely different challenge from writing a book. Everything has to be mapped out: the learning objectives, the lesson flow, the worksheets, the assessments, the grading criteria, and the outcomes you want students to walk away with. I have been working on a curriculum since earlier this year and I am still refining it even at 95 percent complete. This is not something you start on a whim. It requires research, experience, patience, and a deep commitment to the subject matter.

> *A book opens the door. A curriculum walks through it. Build the foundation first and the next level of impact will follow naturally.*

## The Vision: Pouring Into the Next Generation

Everything I am doing as an author, as a curriculum developer, as a creative entrepreneur, comes back to one core belief: people need to think for themselves and too many of them have never been taught how. I am consistently amazed at how many adults lack critical thinking skills. That is the space I am moving into more deeply with every project I take on.

## A Personal Word to You

I want to close this book by speaking directly to you, the person who picked this up because you have a book inside of you and you were not sure how to get it out.

You now have the roadmap. You know how to structure your book, design your cover, format your interior, purchase your ISBN, publish through IngramSpark, price your work, market it, and keep building beyond that first title. You have everything you need to start and finish your first book correctly.

What I want you to take from my story, beyond the technical steps, is this: a book is proof. It is proof that you took your knowledge seriously. It is proof that you showed up for your own ideas. Publishing a book changes how the world sees you, but more importantly it changes how you see yourself. And that shift, from someone who wants to write a book to someone who has written one, is more powerful than most people realize until they are standing on the other side of it.

I published my first book without all the information in this guide. I made mistakes, I corrected them, and I kept going. You have a significant advantage over where I started. Use it.

**Now go write your book.**

---

*You have the knowledge. You have the roadmap. The only thing left is to begin.*

---

## Final Reflection: Your Author Vision

**1. What do you want people to say about you because you wrote this book?**

2. Beyond this first book, what other books do you see yourself
writing?



3. Who is one person in your life who needs to read the book
you are about to write?



4. What is your commitment date? When will your first draft
be complete?



5. What does your author journey look like five years from
now?

# Resources and Recommended Tools

- Canva Pro: canva.com

- Bowker ISBN: myidentifiers.com

- IngramSpark: ingramspark.com

- Amazon Author Central: author.amazon.com

- IngramSpark Cover Template Generator: available at ingramspark.com

# Other Books by Char Vernon

- Practice Makes Perfect: Alphabetical Tracing Workbook
- Brandon's Brave Biking Bonanza
- The Curious Adventures of Kiki in the Kitchen
- A to Z: A Day at the Park with Friends
- Ava's Amazing Alphabet Adventure
- Make That Sh*t Happen: 30 Day Good Habits Journal
- Launch and Thrive: Step by Step Side Hustle Guide
- Navigating the Workforce While Black in America
- The Struggles in Today's Job Market
- Manifest Like a Misfit: A 30-Day Manifestation Journal

# About the Author

Char Vernon is an author, HR professional, and creative entrepreneur with over 25 years of experience in human resources, executive support, and workforce strategy. She holds a Master's degree in Human Resource Management and is currently pursuing her Doctorate in Communications, combining real-world expertise with advanced academic insight.

As the founder of Visionary Consults, LLC, Char creates practical tools, career resources, and engaging content designed to empower individuals to navigate both professional and personal challenges with confidence.

Her body of work spans multiple genres, from workforce development guides like 2025 is a Shhh Show: The Struggles in Today's Job Market to imaginative children's books such as Brandon's Brave Biking Bonanza. Her children's stories blend rhythm, creativity, and life lessons, encouraging resilience, critical thinking, and confidence in young readers.

From her first publication to a growing catalog of books and resources, Char's work reflects continuous growth, authenticity, and a commitment to creating meaningful, impactful content.

Learn more at VisionaryConsults.org.